The Making of Americans
An Opera and a Play
by Leon Katz

From the Novel by Gertrude Stein

1973

Something Else Press, *Inc.*

Barton   Brownington   Berlin

The Making of Americans

An Opera and a Play

Words and phrases from Gertrude Stein's *Notebooks* are used by permission of the Estate of Gertrude Stein and also by permission of The Gertrude Stein Collection, *Collection of American Literature, Beinecke Rare Book and Manuscript Library, Yale University.*

Cover photograph of Gertrude Stein was taken in the studio at rue de Fleurus, c. 1905, and is used by permission of Edward Burns.

The Making of Americans, An Opera and a Play, From the Novel by Gertrude Stein was first performed at Judson Poets' Theater (on the occasion of its tenth anniversary) during the Fall of 1972, and was directed by Lawrence Kornfeld. The musical score was written by Al Carmines and is available for production from his agent, Arthur Zinberg, 11 West 44th Street, New York, N.Y. 10017.

L. C. CATALOG CARD NO.: 73-76850
ISBN: 0-87110-108-4 (cloth) and 0-87110-110-6 (paper)

Manufactured in the United States of America.

Act One

Act I
Scene 1

Gertrude Stein

(Alone)

I write for myself and strangers
This is the only way that I can do it
No one who knows me can like it
I want readers so strangers must do it

There are many that I know and they know it
They are all of them repeating and I hear it
I love it and I tell it, I love it and now I will write it

I write for myself and strangers
This is now a little of what I love and how I write it

(The scene has become visible. Grandmother Martha, Grandfather David, *their* Children, *in* Grandfather David's *butcher shop.* Grandfather David *sits to one side, on a stool.* Grand-

MOTHER MARTHA *and the* CHILDREN *are at the counter and at a chopping block, ready to cut, wrap and sell)*

GRANDFATHER DAVID

Eating and a quiet life

GERTRUDE STEIN

Grandfather David

GRANDFATHER DAVID

To sit and think
To be important in religion

GERTRUDE STEIN

His gentle nature

GRANDFATHER DAVID

Martha and the children

GERTRUDE STEIN

His blue eyes, his lightish colored beard

GRANDFATHER DAVID

Mostly liking all the world

GERTRUDE STEIN

Grandfather David. He could not lead

GRANDFATHER DAVID

All right, I will go
Yes to be sure it will be very nice there
Only it is very nice here
The village, the shop, the children
Yes, all right, perhaps
Maybe she is right
There is no reason
All right

(GRANDMOTHER MARTHA *approaches him*)

GERTRUDE STEIN

Back straight, flat and firmly supporting

GRANDFATHER DAVID

All right, I will go, all right
My Martha can fix it any way she likes it
Yes it will be nice to have all of them get rich there
All right we will go
To America

GERTRUDE STEIN

Strong to bear many children and always after strong to lead
them.

GRANDFATHER DAVID

But it is very nice here
Religion, the village, the shop
And everything I have known all my life here
All right, we will go
We will all go and get rich there
Martha can fix it any way she likes it
It will be good for the children to have it

All right we will all go
All right my Martha can fix it
All right if she wants to do it
I will go, all right, I will go

GERTRUDE STEIN

Strong and good and directing. Grandmother Martha

(The FAMILY *dismantles the shop, and things from
it are put on a wagon. During this action:)*

I write down a little each day
Here on my scraps of paper
For you
My reader
Can there ever be for me any such a creature
No
This scribbled and dirty and lined paper

Is to be to me always my receiver
Anyhow
Reader
Arm yourself to be patient and to be eager
And wait while I hasten slowly forwards
And love please this history
Of a decent family's progress

(As the FAMILY *journeys, the* CHILDREN *sing)*

THE CHILDREN

Many little times of tired
Many ways of being tired
Between the first hot sense of tired
And the last dead tired sense that is so tired

The dull drag of being almost dead with being tired
You cannot press through to a new strength and another tired
You keep on, you keep on when you have learned how to do it
You harden to it and know there is no pressing through it
There is no way to win out beyond it, it is just a dreary dull
    dead tired
You learn to know it, and it is always, and you learn to bear it
The dull drag of being almost dead with being tired

GERTRUDE STEIN

Grandfather David had done it
He had slipped back and they had lost him

GRANDMOTHER MARTHA
(When THEY *have stopped:)*
He is sitting at the first turning
Looking at the village below him

GERTRUDE STEIN
Looking at the village below him
At all the things he was leaving
And he simply could not endure it in him

GRANDMOTHER MARTHA
You go on
Keep on slowly
I go back to get him

(As SHE *walks back, the* CHILDREN *go on)*

THE CHILDREN
Hot trudging, when every step has its conscious meaning
And all the movement is as if one were lifting each muscle and
    every part of the skin as a separate action
A weary conscious moving the way it is before you press
    through it to the time of steady walking

*(*GRANDMOTHER MARTHA *has reached* GRANDFATHER
DAVID, *who is sitting on the same stool)*

GRANDMOTHER MARTHA

I never want you not to do everything just like you really need
  it
You just say David what you want and I do it

GRANDFATHER DAVID

I just came back here to see it
I go on with you now I got a look to see I don't forget it
I just stopped here to see it
Alright we go now I done what I needed

Now we go on to do it like we said we would do it
I just looked to see I got it fixed right so I don't forget it

GRANDMOTHER MARTHA

You just say David what you want to be doing
David I say you just say what you want and we do it

GRANDFATHER DAVID

It is hard to start but it is harder to keep going
I just stopped here to see it

(GRANDMOTHER MARTHA *and* GRANDFATHER DAVID
move toward the CHILDREN *and the wagon)*

THE CHILDREN
(Continuing)

Settling to it, the steady walking, not any longer with a
    conscious sense of any movement
Becoming really strong to do it
Now just coming to it
Just pressing through the first hot tired

GRANDMOTHER MARTHA

Too hot for you David to do so much walking
You should not do any more walking
It will be better, when we come to the wagon, if you would
    get in
And ride a little with the little children
Not to get sick, and nobody to take care of us
The only one that can do our talking

(*THEY have reached the wagon, and* GRANDFATHER
DAVID *has been mounted on top of it, riding above
them all*)

GRANDMOTHER MARTHA

Until we come to the city by the water
And the ship to take us to the new world

GERTRUDE STEIN

And soon it was too far
And then he had the new city, and the ship
And then he had the new world around him

And then he was content

ACT I
SCENE 2

The wagon and its contents are formed into a large, almost throne-like seat, enclosed within an arch, and a canopy for a Jewish wedding. Boxes are put about for seats and tables.

GERTRUDE STEIN

Old people in a new world
New people made out of the old

Our grandmothers carried our mothers and fathers
Into the new world inside them
These women of the old world strong to bear them

(The stage is dark. FOUR OLD WOMEN *are spotlighted)*

17

These four women
There was one
Her passion

FIRST GRANDMOTHER

Strong to bear many children
And then always strong to suffer with them

GERTRUDE STEIN

There was one
Her dreary trickling

SECOND GRANDMOTHER

Strong to bear many children
Then always after sadly suffer for them
Weeping for the sadness of all sinning
Weary for the rest my death will bring them

GERTRUDE STEIN

There was one
Her sweetness

THIRD GRANDMOTHER

Strong just to bear many children
Then to die away and leave them
That is all I know to do for them

GERTRUDE STEIN

There was one
Her strength

GRANDMOTHER MARTHA

Strong to bear many children
Then always very strong to lead them

(The stage is dark again. Only GERTRUDE STEIN *is
visible)*

GERTRUDE STEIN

Kinds of men and women
And the children they had with them

Some, poor things, who never learned to make a living
Some who dreamed while others fought a way to help them
Some whose children went to pieces with them
Some who thought and thought
And then their children rose to greatness through them

Children, children's children
Wandering over the new land
Seeking first just to make a living
Some later to grow rich
Some later to gain wisdom

And we
Realizing now
How they slowly came to make us

*(*DAVID HERSLAND, *dressed as groom, appears in spotlight, seated)*

Realizing our fathers
To know ourselves

DAVID HERSLAND

Between myself and everything existing
There is not any difference

GERTRUDE STEIN

David Hersland

DAVID HERSLAND

Big as all the world
As all the world around me

(FANNY HISSEN, *dressed as bride, appears in spotlight.* SHE *is sitting on the throne-like seat*)

GERTRUDE STEIN

Slowly knowing our mothers and fathers
To know ourselves

FANNY HISSEN

To live and die in mildness and contentment

GERTRUDE STEIN

Fanny Hissen

FANNY HISSEN

To be gently important in living

GERTRUDE STEIN

The so fine weakness in her
The gentle dignity that made her

> *(Lights come up full. The bustle of a big Jewish wed-
> ding, 1864.* DAVID HERSLAND *in the center of a group
> of* MEN *who are, like himself, middle-aged.* FANNY
> HISSEN, *enthroned, surrounded by a group of* WOM-
> EN. GRANDFATHER DAVID, *in black silk suit and tallit,
> sitting to one side, his ruminations interrupted when*
> GUESTS *come forward to congratulate him on his son's
> wedding.* MARTHA, DAVID HERSLAND'S *matchmaking
> sister, is the energetic center of the wedding)*

THE GUESTS

Marrying is only loving
That is American teaching
It is loving that is strong
To make a real beginning
Marrying is only loving
American teaching
Marrying is all loving
American teaching

GRANDFATHER DAVID
(Sitting to one side)

Yes, all right
And I say it to them
But it is all too new to my feeling
It can never be a comfort to me
It is all always too new

SISTER MARTHA

American teaching is lying
That says it is all loving
That is strong to make a beginning

GERTRUDE STEIN

Sister Martha

SISTER MARTHA

When the man is fixed in his way of living
When he finds it pleasant to go on as he is doing
It is then not enough that he feels a little loving
It takes then his sister

GERTRUDE STEIN

Her important feeling

SISTER MARTHA

It takes then his sister
Or the girl herself if she is strong
To do the work of winning
To get the man really ripe for marrying

GERTRUDE STEIN

Her keeping strongly to it
Her doing what was right to do
In her feeling

GRANDFATHER DAVID

It is all always too new
My Martha was good
She stayed always beside me
But she died away and left me

SISTER MARTHA

Coaxing, arranging, flattering, teasing
A little good tempered irritated forcing
And then he must see her very often
Or else he will forget all about his loving
And when he is drifting
He must be brought back out of his forgetting

Or else how would there be the right kind of marrying
How would there come to be existing
The decent, honest enough, comfortable men and women
With the not very lively sense in them of loving
And their easy forgetting

GRANDFATHER DAVID

He was a good boy to me always, David
But he never does anything like I tell him
Alright, it ain't wrong in him, never
Only I, I don't need it any more
Just to go on like I was living

(The wedding ceremony begins. DAVID HERSLAND
and FANNY HISSEN *are under the canopy.* SISTER
MARTHA *and* GRANDFATHER DAVID *sit on opposite
sides of stage, watching at a distance)*

SISTER MARTHA

It takes the sister
Who has strongly inside her the need
That all the world keep on going
Who has strongly inside her the sense
Of the rich right way of living

GRANDFATHER DAVID

Going to the far west
It is just beginning to work in him
Maybe marrying might keep him from going

Sister Martha
(To the music of the ceremony)

Men go drifting
Doing a little loving
And then a little forgetting
And then restarting
Until they get so strongly the feeling of loving
With the right kind of helping
That then it is an effort for them
To begin again with their forgetting
And then they are ripe for marrying

Grandfather David

Always
They got some new place to go
To do it different
Alright
It will be good for him
To have a good wife
To be in the far west with him

Sister Martha

Then one of the family of women has him
And marrying contents him
And he has the right kind of living for him
And everything keeps on as it was in the beginning

*(DAVID HERSLAND stomps on the glass. The ceremony
is over. Celebration)*

THE GUESTS

Middle-class, middle-class
No one among you to admit it
No one among you to belong to it
Sordid and material
Unillusioned unaspiring
Monotonous for it is always there
Monotonous, always to be repeated
Yet we are strong and we are right and we know it
We say it, and all must listen to it
That a solid middle-class who know they are it
With their tight bond of family to control it
With no fine kind of fancy ways inside it
With no excitements to surprise it
With no new ways of being bad or good to win it
Is the one thing always right and worthy it
Worthy that all monotonously repeat it
From which has always sprung
And all who really look can see it
The very best the world can ever know
And everywhere we always need it

GRANDFATHER DAVID

Yes, alright, only now
I got nothing to say to my children
Yes, alright, only now
To be left out of all life
Alright, yes, alright
But I, I am still living

(DAVID HERSLAND *and* FANNY HISSEN *embrace*)

DAVID HERSLAND

A flower
But mostly a woman

Act I
Scene 3

DAVID HERSLAND *and* FANNY HERSLAND *are in traveling clothes, with suitcases.* GRANDFATHER DAVID *is still in his suit and tallit. The boxes are stacked center stage, a blank wall.*

GRANDFATHER DAVID
You do not know if you should go

FANNY HERSLAND
Is it wrong for us to do this thing

DAVID HERSLAND
(To his WIFE, *impatiently)*
Let us go

FANNY HERSLAND

When we were children
Shut up with my father
We would not do this thing
Without asking

GRANDFATHER DAVID

My dear child
There was a rabbi
A good man
Someone came to him and said
Can I do this thing
Can I go to the barber on the Sabbath
Is it wrong to do this thing

The rabbi said he forbid him
He must not go on the Sabbath
And get a man to shave him
It would be in him a sin

Then a little later
The man met the rabbi
Coming from the shop
Shaved all fresh and clean

But how is this
You told me when I asked you
That I should not do this thing
It would be for me a sin

Ah, said the rabbi that was right
I told you I forbid you
It would be for you a sin
But I did not do any asking

(THEY *leave.* HE *looks after them)*

GRANDFATHER DAVID

Grown men and women
Married and grown
They are not shut up in my house
I, I am no longer leading

(HE *sits)*

GERTRUDE STEIN

Now he was himself for himself
All there was of living
All there was of religion

GRANDFATHER DAVID

Grown
None shut up with me in my house

GERTRUDE STEIN

And religion was all there was of living

GRANDFATHER DAVID

To go on
To be strong
Myself inside myself

GERTRUDE STEIN

And slowly
In his dying
It was a great death that met him

GRANDFATHER DAVID

All there is of religion

GERTRUDE STEIN

He was religion
Death could not rob him
He could lose nothing in his dying

GRANDFATHER DAVID

All there is of living

GERTRUDE STEIN

And religion was all there was of living

GRANDFATHER DAVID

To be firm
To allow
All of power in myself

GERTRUDE STEIN

So he
Dying of old age
Without struggling
Met himself by himself in his dying

GRANDFATHER DAVID

Everlasting
Without ending

GERTRUDE STEIN

He and religion and living and dying
Were all one and everything and everyone

GRANDFATHER DAVID

Myself inside myself. One

GERTRUDE STEIN

Living, dying, being and religion

ACT I
SCENE 4

*The blank wall of boxes is overturned by the three Hersland children—*YOUNG MARTHA, ALFRED *and* DAVID. *Amid the scattering of boxes,* THEY *lie down, play, tumble.* THEY *are in an open field. Their mother,* FANNY HERSLAND, *sits on far side of stage, not with them.*

FANNY HERSLAND

How can they be so perfect and so wonderful

GERTRUDE STEIN

In the new world of a new world
The newest part of the new world
In half-country, half-city daily living
Each one growing up to be strong
Each one to himself inside him
Finding his way to be free

35

FANNY HERSLAND

So perfect and so wonderful and yet
All three so different from the others of them
Hardly anything alike in the three of them

GERTRUDE STEIN

Big children, and she a very little mother to them
Not knowing what they needed in them
Not ever very important to them
Big children, never very loving to her inside them

FANNY HERSLAND

So perfect and so wonderful

YOUNG MARTHA, ALFRED & DAVID

Wonderful in summer
With the dry heat and the sun burning
And the hot earth for sleeping
Very wonderful

Very pleasant lying down
Watching birds in the black sunlight and sailing
And the firm white summer clouds
Breaking away from the horizon and slowly moving

Good in the summer for generous sweating
Helping the men make hay into bales
For its preserving
And well for ones growing

Eating radishes pulled with the black earth sticking to them
And chewing the mustard
And finding the roots
With all kinds of funny flavors in them

And filling ones hat with fruit
And sitting on the dry ploughed ground
And eating and thinking and sleeping and reading and dreaming
And never hearing when they would all be calling

And when the quail come
Going shooting
And when the wind and the rain and the ground
Are ready to help seeds in their growing
And the wind is so strong
It is blowing the leaves and branches of the trees down around
    you
The trees hitting their own wood
And making that queer sound that you get to have inside you
And the owls in the walls scaring you with their tumbling
And shouting and working and getting wet and being all
    soaking
And running out full in the strong wind and letting it dry you
In between the gusts of rain that leave you soaking
Feeling the strong wind blowing
And real country living
Giving the gusts of rain
And the strong wind blowing
A right feeling
Wonderful

FANNY HERSLAND

So perfect and so wonderful

GERTRUDE STEIN

Big in themselves and in their way of winning
Growing up to be strong
Each one to be free inside him

ACT I
SCENE 5

GERTRUDE STEIN
(Alone)

Slowly telling the history of each of them
Slowly telling how each one
Was important to himself inside him
Slowly how they won a kind of freedom for themselves
Each one inside him

Slowly remembering western living
Half-city, half-country outdoors living

(On one side of stage, lights come up on the HERS-
LAND FAMILY sitting in a room, with outside orchard
indicated. THEY are frozen in position)

Slowly realizing eastern living
Rich solid right american living

*(On the other side of stage, lights come up on the
DEHNING FAMILY—the parents HENRY and JENNY
DEHNING, the children JULIA and GEORGE—sitting
in a room, its splendor of marble and gilt indicated.
THEY are frozen in position)*

And later, much later
Realizing the history
Of the beginning of the middle living
And the loving and the marrying
Of Alfred Hersland and Julia Dehning

Later, much later
The living and the marrying of them

  *(ALFRED HERSLAND and JULIA DEHNING, forward
  of their respective groups, are spotlighted)*

Slowly remembering Hersland living
Slowly remembering Dehning living
Who later will be mixing up in marrying

To begin then

  *(The lights dim slightly on the HERSLANDS, come up
  full on the DEHNINGS)*

JULIA & GEORGE DEHNING
Marbles and bronzes and crystal
Ceiling of angels and cupids
Paintings of well washed peasants
Gas logs in every room

Good solid riches in the Dehning house
And always everywhere
Complicated ways to wash
And dressing tables filled with sponges
Instruments and ways to make one clean

Good solid riches in the Dehning house
Rich nervous luxury living

> *(Lights dim slightly on* DEHNINGS, *come up full on*
> HERSLANDS*)*

MR. DAVID HERSLAND
(Shouting at his THREE CHILDREN, FANNY HERS-
LAND *to one side, not included)*
I know how to make you do

GERTRUDE STEIN
Doing very hard pounding on the table

MR. HERSLAND
I am the father
I am master
You are the children

GERTRUDE STEIN

Shouting and pounding on the table

MR. HERSLAND

Hardening children is the way to do
Everyone should make his own beginning
Everyone should win his own freedom
Fathers must harden their children
That is the right way to do
I know it and I will do it
That is the only way for me to do

ALFRED HERSLAND
(Shouting and pounding)

Always making us ashamed

MR. HERSLAND

What what

ALFRED HERSLAND

Ashamed
When all the people are looking and wondering and laughing
And giving you a name for the queer ways in you
Making us ashamed to say
You are the father to us
When other children laugh about you
We are ashamed

MR. HERSLAND

You are the mother
You will stop this
I, I will go

ALFRED HERSLAND

No
Now you will hear it
You have no right to do such acting
You started us in this way of doing
Youve got no right to change it now

MR. HERSLAND

I will stop this
I will stop this

ALFRED HERSLAND

You think you are not fearful
You think you tell and say
And that is all the strength you need
To give to us our way of living

MR. HERSLAND

What

ALFRED HERSLAND

Always brushing us away from around you
When you do not know how to go through
And when you cannot keep us brushed down from in front of
   you
You go another way
And never know
That you are a coward in you then in living

MRS. HERSLAND

I will stop this

(Lights dim a little on HERSLANDS, *come up full on*
DEHNINGS)

HENRY DEHNING

Horses and teachers and music and tutors
And all kinds of modern improvements
Well! What! Yes you children have an easy time of it
Nowadays
Doing nothing

*(*GEORGE *and* JULIA *laugh)*

GERTRUDE STEIN

Proud of all the things
He knew that they could teach him

HENRY DEHNING
(With good humor)

No you children
Will never be good for something

Modern improvements

GERTRUDE STEIN

Henry Dehning
Challenging them
Liking it
They liking it in him

HENRY DEHNING

What, well, alright, I say
I am good and ready to sit still and watch
To see how you all do it

JULIA & GEORGE DEHNING
(Laughing)

You will see, you will see
Alright, you just wait and see

HENRY DEHNING

I say I am waiting now

GERTRUDE STEIN

And the sharp, narrow, outward look
That, closing him
Went very straight into them

JULIA & GEORGE DEHNING

It will be different
But I guess we will be good for something

GERTRUDE STEIN

But always a little dread in them
Deep down, the fear
Perhaps he really knows
That look so outward from him
An old mans sharp looking

GEORGE DEHNING

Youll see, we will be good for something

GERTRUDE STEIN

The burr in the voice that makes for terror in the children
A sharp, narrow, outward, shut off glance from an old man
That fills with dread young grown men and women

Mostly for all children
And young grown men and women
There is much terror in an old mans looking

GEORGE DEHNING

We will be good for something

(Lights dim on DEHNINGS, *come up full on* HERS-LANDS)*

MR. HERSLAND
(To ALFRED*)*

Martha should not go out in the evening
She should not stay so much with the poor people near us
That is no way for a daughter of mine
In my position
Should be acting

I forbid her going
She must stay in the house with her mother
And you
You must take better care of your sister
You are the oldest

ALFRED HERSLAND

She is the oldest

MR. HERSLAND

You are the oldest son
And she is only a girl

You have to take care of her sometime
And you might as well begin
The sooner the better
You have to do it sooner or later

ALFRED HERSLAND

Ill take mine later

MR. HERSLAND

What

ALFRED HERSLAND

On Sundays when you walk
And stop to talk to them
And sit down in the houses with the women when they are
   cooking
And feel inside you a nice feeling that there are women there
   in the room with you
Then you say it is a good thing
Martha should learn how to do things
Cooking and sewing and living like the poor women you are
   seeing
Then you say Martha should learn the living they have in them
Now you are changing
Why. Because it is not Sunday

MR. HERSLAND

I tell you she will not go out of an evening
I tell you
I will see to it that she should stay home
And I will hire someone to look after her

And make her the kind of educated person
That it is right that I
A man in my position
Should have for a daughter

Ah you see
That is it
What do I want for my children
A real governess
A foreign woman with governess training
One who is a good musician
Music is something everyone should have in their living
One who will talk french and german with my children
That is what I want to have for my children
That is the right way to do
I know it and I will do it
That is the only way for me to do

You are the mother
You will see to it
                              (HE *leaves*.

Lights dim on HERSLANDS, *come up on* DEHNINGS)

HENRY DEHNING
Younger than Julia here
And my brother no bigger than George
And we left home to make our way here

JENNY DEHNING

Loving to remember
And telling it over
And most often to the children
What he has been
And what he has done
And how he himself has made it all so different

HENRY DEHNING

Waiting in a big bare room
For them to give us tickets
And hearing some one say our fathers name
Not daring then to speak
Not knowing who it was that knew us

JENNY DEHNING

He says it long
And he says it often
But it is never any more now
Present to his feeling
He has it all and only
Like a dim beginning

But they are afraid
But they always stay and listen to him
But he does not listen to them
He goes on telling what he has done
And what he thinks of them

HENRY DEHNING

We were ten
And she made our clothes
And did her washing
And in between made peppermint candy
For the little ones to sell

JENNY DEHNING

But I never listen to him
I am deaf to him
Or go away when he begins this kind of talking
                    (SHE *leaves*)

HENRY DEHNING

Learning working hard
And selling candy
And monkeys on a stick
And anything we could do

(JENNY DEHNING *returns*)

JENNY DEHNING

But proud of him
I do not forget the way he has come
And proud that he himself has done it
His power
And all he has
And the honest way that he has done it

But always doing little things so badly
And still always playing like a poor man with his fingers

Not proud of the way he is
But proud of the way he has come

HENRY DEHNING
O Miss Jenny, she is the best girl I know
Too good for you, thats all
Giving you what will never help
To make you good for something

JENNY DEHNING
Not too good a woman, but a good woman
Not a bad one
Harsh in any attacking
But he, my Henry, is not gentle
Only smoother in resisting

HENRY DEHNING
(*Embracing her*)
Miss Jenny, she is the best girl I know

JENNY DEHNING
Dont do that, Henry
(SHE *leaves*)

GERTRUDE STEIN
(As JENNY DEHNING *is leaving)*
Hitting the ground with the same hard jerk
With which she rebuked him for his sins
A woman generous and honest
One whom one might like the better
The more one saw her less

HENRY DEHNING
(Circling about, with a dancing motion)
O Miss Jenny is the best girl I know

(Lights dim on DEHNINGS, *come up on* HERSLANDS.
MR. HERSLAND *and his* CHILDREN *are at the table
playing cards;* FANNY HERSLAND *sits to one side, not
with them)*

MR. HERSLAND
(Jumping up from the card table)
Finish, finish
You are the mother
Finish playing with them

ALFRED HERSLAND
You started this playing
We did not want to play
We are only playing for you

MR. HERSLAND

Finish, finish
I will watch

(FANNY HERSLAND *sits with them, and* THEY *play.*
MR. HERSLAND *paces, glances at their playing, goes
out, comes back eating, while* THEY *are playing)*

MARTHA HERSLAND
(While playing)

Just like him
But never having it to understand him
Never finishing, like him
But never filling with impatient feeling then
Not like him

Always irritating him
Always then afraid of the irritation in him
That I always give to him
Having it to be like him
But never having it to understand him

ALFRED HERSLAND
(While playing)

Not like him
Not beginning strong like him
No such big beginning in me
Not like him

Seeing the big beginnings in him
Wanting so much myself such big beginnings
Loving so much the big ways in him
Fills me with impatient feeling
Just like him

Feeling the joyous bigness always in him
Wanting to have it too inside of me

YOUNG DAVID HERSLAND

Not like him
Big as all the world inside me, yes
But not like him

One day
All the world around me
And all the world inside me
Will be
In my understanding
One

One day
The world will be
Myself inside myself
In whole whole understanding
One

Not like him
Who can never understand me
Not like him

His always beginning
And always filling with impatient feeling
Is always, to me, failing

For his always beginning
And then always failing
There is always a little, in me, of contempt

MR. HERSLAND

Is it finished

ALFRED HERSLAND
(Throwing down his cards and shouting furiously)
No, not finished

MR. HERSLAND
(Shouting furiously)

I will stop this

(HE leaves.

*The OTHERS, except for ALFRED, jump up from the
card table and go to different parts of the room, saying
nothing)*

ALFRED HERSLAND

The more I shout and pound
The more I am like him

GERTRUDE STEIN

Once an angry man
Dragged his father along the ground
Through his own orchard

ALFRED HERSLAND

The more I shout and pound
The more I am like him

GERTRUDE STEIN

Stop, cried the old man, stop
I did not drag my father

ALFRED HERSLAND

The more I shout and pound
The more I am like him

GERTRUDE STEIN

Beyond this tree

ALFRED HERSLAND

The more I shout and pound

(Lights dim on HERSLANDS, *come up on* DEHNINGS.

GEORGE *and* JULIA DEHNING *are on the floor, on their
stomachs, thumbing books.* HENRY DEHNING *stands,
studies the room, his* CHILDREN)

HENRY DEHNING

I stand and look about
Yes truly, it is now all very different with me
Children so prosperous, good-looking, honest
And always respectful to me
And what! well, yes, so fine hope of winning for themselves
All that I could ever wish to them

Can one ever have it real to him
That in one life time
A man could have it all so different for him
That a man all alone
In a single life time
Could make it so that he could have it to be
Truly
All so different for him

No, for a man to have it so different
In a single life time
Is more strange than being born
And being then a baby
And then a child
And then a young grown man
And then old like a man grown old
And then dead and so no more of living
It is more strange
Because it makes so many lives
In this one living

I forget and I remember
Many dim beginnings in me
And so many lives I have had
To my feeling
In me
In my living

END OF ACT ONE

Act Two

Act II
Scene 1

Gertrude Stein

(Alone)

The way I have been telling
Is not the way

Characters in times and places
What are they
No, for realizing men and women
Events and times and places
Are not the way

It is hard to know the being in any one
From just description of some thoughts
Of some feelings
Of some actions
In them

For the kind of being in them
Shows in them
Only from the feeling of themselves inside them

61

And that comes out of them slowly
Always in their living
That comes out of them slowly
Always as repeating

It is very very hard
To make any one understand
The being in them
From description of them

It is very very hard
And sometime sometimes
Someone else will know
All I know of this
By my explaining

I am never very certain
But again and again there is
Again and again for me
A beginning of this trying

Now I will begin again
Now always realising
The feeling of themselves to themselves
Inside them

    (ALFRED HERSLAND *is visible, alone, in spotlight*)

I am waiting now to realize Alfred Hersland
To himself inside him

ALFRED HERSLAND
(Softly—not yet realized)

When the eldest son
Is not the oldest one
It is not a pleasant thing

GERTRUDE STEIN

I am waiting to realize the being
Of Alfred Hersland in his young living

ALFRED HERSLAND

I am the eldest son
I am not the oldest one

When a woman a girl a sister is the older one
When you are the oldest son
It is not such a pleasant thing

GERTRUDE STEIN

I am waiting to be full up
With the kind of them
All there are of that kind of them
Who are like Alfred Hersland

I am very completely full
I am quite completely full
Of the kind of being there is in Alfred Hersland

I am waiting to be a fuller one
I am waiting to be full up
With that kind of being

I am now
As I am saying
Waiting

> *(The stage lights up full.* ALFRED HERSLAND *is surrounded by* YOUNG CHILDREN. THEY *play)*

THE CHILDREN
Arthur Banks, George Banks, Albert Banks, Frank Roddy, Will
Roddy, Louis Champion, Henry Fisher, Mary Fisher, Cora
Fisher, James Henry, Henry Henry, Rose Henry, Carrie Henry

Doing roller skating
Doing a little shooting
Doing some camping
A good deal of fishing
Picking fruit from the Hersland orchard
Going about the country selling fruit

Carrie Henry, Rose Henry, Henry Henry, James Henry

GERTRUDE STEIN
I am waiting to realize children
I am waiting to realize childhood in Alfred Hersland
I am waiting and I am not yet certain
I am not yet impatient yet in waiting
I am going I think very soon to be keeping on going

THE CHILDREN
Being in a vacant lot playing
Or hanging around together somewhere
And often enough chasing around in the Hersland garden

GERTRUDE STEIN
I am completely always nearer understanding
And yet there are some problems I am feeling
I am very full up now with this kind of them
The Alfred Hersland kind of them
Still I am feeling problems in completion
They are not yet to me entirely completely yet
Whole ones inside me

ALFRED HERSLAND
(Sings very softly as the OTHER CHILDREN *move slowly and quietly.* HE *ends in mid-phrase, like a music-box, run down)*
Albert Banks, George Banks, Arthur Banks, Carrie Henry, Rose Henry, Henry Hen. . .

*(*THEY ALL *stop; freeze in position)*

GERTRUDE STEIN
I am not now going on with Alfred Hersland
I will wait in another direction

(Blackout on ALL *but* MARTHA HERSLAND*)*

Act II
Scene 2

MARTHA *is holding an umbrella and begins to run.*

GERTRUDE STEIN
This one was a very little one then
And she was running and she was in the street
And it was a muddy one
And she had an umbrella that she was dragging
And she was crying

MARTHA HERSLAND
I will throw the umbrella in the mud

GERTRUDE STEIN
She was very little then
She was just beginning her schooling

MARTHA HERSLAND

I will throw the umbrella in the mud

GERTRUDE STEIN

And no one was near her
And she was dragging the umbrella
And bitterness possessed her

MARTHA HERSLAND

I will throw the umbrella in the mud

GERTRUDE STEIN

And nobody heard her
Her brothers had run ahead to get home
And they had left her

MARTHA HERSLAND

I will throw the umbrella in the mud

GERTRUDE STEIN

And she was telling and nobody was hearing
And there was desperate anger in her

MARTHA HERSLAND

I have throwed the umbrella in the mud

GERTRUDE STEIN

She had thrown the umbrella in the mud
And that was the end of it all in her
She had thrown the umbrella in the mud
And no one heard her as it burst from her

MARTHA HERSLAND

I have throwed the umbrella in the mud

GERTRUDE STEIN

It was the end of all that to her

Martha Hersland
She was a very little one then
And she wanted not to be existing

(MARTHA *remains on the ground, weeping*)
Sometimes I want to turn away
So that I will not know it too clearly in them
The being that they have in them

A little now I want to turn away
In looking at the being in this one
It gives to me seeing her an uncomfortable feeling
To know the meaning of the being so well in this one

(BERTHA, fat and buttery, enters, stands in spotlight)
This one I am now bringing in
Does not belong to our story
She is only Bertha, who is my older sister
Soon we will lose her

I just want to show now
How Martha Hersland was made like this one
Only more concentrated
More consistent
In her being

BERTHA

This one is one
This one is a whole one
This one is a mushy mass of being

GERTRUDE STEIN

Sister Bertha

BERTHA

Completely fluid inside
With only a skin to hold it all together
To keep it separate from the world
And from flowing over everything

GERTRUDE STEIN

To know it so well
Makes one turn away from seeing

BERTHA

Slow in action
Barely in motion

So slow in attacking
That it looks like resisting

GERTRUDE STEIN

This one is very existing to my feeling

BERTHA

Action starting
Slowly wobbling
Mass of stupid being

The same whole one
All my living
To myself and every one

GERTRUDE STEIN

Sister Bertha
Undifferentiated mass
(Speaking)
This one is then the simplest form of her kind of being.
Everyone having in them anything of this kind of being is
connected with this one then.

BERTHA & MARTHA
(Singing together)

Each one is one
Each one is like another one
Each one is of a kind in men and women
And there are many millions of each kind of them

GERTRUDE STEIN
(As BERTHA *waddles off)*

This is the being then in Martha Hersland
Bertha's bottom being
Bertha's mushy mass of being
Bertha's barely in motion being
Bertha's mostly stupid being

Martha Hersland
Bertha with an extra push

MARTHA HERSLAND
(Repeating last action)

I have throwed the umbrella in the mud

(Blackout)

Act II
Scene 3

Singing of the CHILDREN *begins in the dark. Lights come up slowly, during the litany of names, on* AL-FRED HERSLAND *and the* OTHER CHILDREN, *again assembled.*

THE CHILDREN
Cora Fisher, Mary Fisher, Henry Fisher, Will Roddy, Frank Roddy, Louis Champion

We, living now, are always to ourselves
Young grown men and women
When we are very little children
We say then yes we are children
But we know then way inside us
That we are not real as children
We are grown to ourselves, as young grown men and women

GERTRUDE STEIN

Learning, thinking, living in children's being
Often has in it little of real being
Real being, the bottom of them
Often does not do in them
Very loud repeating

THE CHILDREN

And to be old
To be old as old men and women
Once were and still are to our feeling old
No, no one can be old like that
To himself in his feeling

GERTRUDE STEIN

Listening to repeating
Knowing being in every one
Who ever was or is or will be living
Slowly comes to be in me
A louder and a louder pounding

THE CHILDREN

To be old to ourselves is a losing of ourselves
Like just dropping off into sleeping
To be awake we must be to ourselves
Always young grown men and women

GERTRUDE STEIN

I have it in my feeling
To feel all living
To have each one come to be a whole one to me
From his repeating of himself inside him

Listening to repeating
Always more and more
Gives to me completed understanding
Each one slowly comes to be a whole one to me
Each one slowly comes to be a whole one in me

THE CHILDREN

There is no other way to do with our thinking
We to ourselves are always to ourselves
Young grown men and women

GERTRUDE STEIN

Listening to repeating can be tiring
Listen to repeating can be dulling
Sometimes I get irritated by it
Always I love it
Listening to repeating
And each one becoming whole for me
Is all my life
I love it and I live it

I am troubled
Alfred Hersland is in pieces for me
He is still not doing very loud repeating

ALFRED HERSLAND

Not such a pleasant thing
When you are not the oldest one
When you are the eldest son

GERTRUDE STEIN

Alfred Hersland is now in pieces for me
Sometimes one for many years is baffling
I begin again with listening
I stop myself from being quickly sure
I wait for louder beating
I hear new sounds repeating
Slowly it comes to have a fuller pounding
Years can pass in such a baffling listening
Slowly this one comes to have real meaning

ALFRED HERSLAND

The eldest son and not the oldest one
Is not a pleasant thing

GERTRUDE STEIN

Still Alfred Hersland is in pieces for me
I will wait

I will wait a little while now
Before I begin to realize him again

(Lights begin to dim very slowly)

Waiting is always to me interesting
For always something is coming or else nothing is coming
And there is eating sleeping laughing living talking
And a little tickling in the body and the mind
And the drowsiness of going to be lively waking
But always I am nearer to beginning

And now I am content again with waiting

(The stage is in total darkness. A long pause)

Waiting

(A pause)
I will be full up with him
(A pause)
I am still now not going on
(A pause)
I am still now waiting
(A pause)
And that is what I am doing
(A pause)
Waiting

ACT II
SCENE 4

A slow dim-up on YOUNG DAVID HERSLAND, *alone in the* HERSLAND *house. Lights remain dim and murky during this scene.*

GERTRUDE STEIN

In waiting
I will begin to realize
Young David Hersland

DAVID
(Tentatively, very quietly, stopping and starting)
What
I was
Thinking of
Was not
So much

But

GERTRUDE STEIN
(Also very quietly, almost whispering)
His mode of speech
Make it like that

DAVID

Sure
And so
To speak

GERTRUDE STEIN
Make his movement when he talks
Like Leon Solomons
The way Leon did when arguing

Twitch and movement of the hand
All the fingers work together
Have to have them all together
To give them power enough
Work together to reinforce

*(*DAVID's *movement during this evocation of him: as
though in stop-action.)*

(Speaking)
No, I am not in a hurry to begin my hero

*(*DAVID *freezes; stops in mid-action)*

Do not be in a hurry to create him

Leo and Leon and Pablo and me
Combine us all in him

Do not be in a hurry to create him
Make him the complete one
The individual one
Complete

(Lights dim on Hersland *house)*

Act II
Scene 5

GERTRUDE STEIN
There is nothing for it now but to go back to Martha Hersland.

(Lights up full on the HERSLAND *house.* DAVID *lies down on the floor, reading.* MARTHA *comes in and sits on the floor beside him.* ALFRED *comes in and sits at the table, doing homework.* THEY *are now in their teens—about five years older than in previous scene of the Hersland family.*

MARTHA *talks to* DAVID, *but neither* ALFRED *nor* DAVID *pay any attention to her)*

Martha Hersland
Not an interesting one, but a whole one

MARTHA HERSLAND
One little boy wanted to do loving
It was not very much of a success

83

I had a nervous feeling
And was not very understanding
There was confusion
A little like wanting
A little like being stubborn
A little like hesitation
A little like being afraid of everything
A little like a stupid way of being

And the little boy Harry Brenner
Who with his sister lives with his father
Who smokes to help him with his asthma
Got up and altogether forgot
About my being existing

It is very hard
Not to be interesting enough
To be successful in loving
Or in quarreling
They all forget then
That I am being
When I want to be quarreling
Or they are quarreling
Or when they want to be loving
Or I want to be loving

It is very hard not being very interesting

One little boy wanted to do loving
I want to be telling that it happened
But my feeling isnt ready yet for telling

                                Gertrude Stein
Of how much she had heard
And how little she knew
In living

   (Blackout)

Act II
Scene 6

GERTRUDE STEIN

Now there must be a beginning
To the real realization in me
Of Alfred Hersland and his living
I have been doing a very great deal of waiting

(Lights come up brilliantly and suddenly on ALFRED
HERSLAND.*)*

Beginning again

What is general
What is concrete

ALFRED HERSLAND

I am general
I am concrete
There is no contradiction
I have in me no complication

GERTRUDE STEIN

What is fear

ALFRED HERSLAND

Fear we are becoming really dead ones
And fear that dead ones are not really dead ones
Fear makes it that we have it in us
That we think we have it in us
That we believe we have religion in us
And virtuous being in us

And always we have it in us
A continuous knowing in us
A concrete knowing in us
To be dead is completely to be dead

GERTRUDE STEIN

What is ecstasy

ALFRED HERSLAND

Ah certainly
To be dead is really to be dead
And so not anything has ever any ending
Everything is going on forever

GERTRUDE STEIN

What is lying

ALFRED HERSLAND

Knowing and believing in no ending
This gives a sweetness to me
This gives upgazing to me
And always I do not know that I am lying

And ah this comes to be
As love in me
As having loving being in me

I have it as loving in me
That nothing is ever ending
I have it as loving being
And own the thing I need for loving

GERTRUDE STEIN

Now I am completely full
With the kind Alfred Hersland is in being

Alfred Hersland has resisting being in him

ALFRED HERSLAND

I do not say that dead is dead
And then not really know for sure
That dead is altogether dead

GERTRUDE STEIN

The resisting kind of men
Engulfing and resisting kind
In men and women

ALFRED HERSLAND

I do not have a different general
And a different concrete thinking
The one thing mixed up with the other thing
I do not, I do not

GERTRUDE STEIN

I am feeling now the temper stirring in Alfred Hersland
The kind of temper he has in him
He has a temper in him that is a common thing
With those having in them
Resisting being tending to the engulfing kind
Alfred Hersland has this kind of angry action

ALFRED HERSLAND
(Angry)

I have a temper
But not that funny kind of temper

GERTRUDE STEIN

Not an angry or a sullen person mostly
But that common kind of temper
Of the engulfing kind

ALFRED HERSLAND
(Very angry)

I do not have that kind of temper
I do not do that kind of lying
I do not

GERTRUDE STEIN
At last he is a whole one to me
At last I am completely full with Alfred Hersland

ALFRED HERSLAND
(Furious)
I do not have that kind of temper

GERTRUDE STEIN
Alfred Hersland
The resisting, the engulfing kind

ALFRED HERSLAND
(Shouting and pounding)
I am not

(Blackout)

ACT II
SCENE 7

The HERSLAND *house.* FANNY HERSLAND *is propped up on the sofa with pillows;* SHE *is ailing.*

MR. HERSLAND *sits at a distance from her, watching her;* HE *gets up and paces from time to time.*

YOUNG DAVID *sits at the table, watching his* PARENTS. HE *is deeply, bitterly reflecting.* HE *wears his coat; his hat lies on the table near him; his suitcase is on the floor beside him.* HE *has slid down in his chair, his feet outstretched, his hands in his overcoat pockets.*

MARTHA *is tending to her* MOTHER, *and serving coffee to her* FATHER.

In this scene, MARTHA *is twenty-three,* ALFRED—*not come in yet—is twenty-one,* DAVID *is seventeen.* MR. HERSLAND *is in his late fifties,* MRS. HERSLAND *in her late forties.*

DAVID
(To himself)

There were two
There were Martha and Alfred
And there were to be three

MR. HERSLAND
(Angrily to MARTHA)

No sugar in my coffee

(MARTHA *takes coffee and goes out*)

DAVID
(To himself)

There were two others dead
Before my being living

MR. HERSLAND
(Angrily to EVERYONE)

I do not take sugar in my coffee

DAVID
(To himself)

Two came one after the other
And they did not go on living

I did not know this thing
I did not know this thing

MR. HERSLAND
(To himself)

Three children
Two are leaving

Anyways for me
Always outside of me
Always part of the world outside of me

MRS. HERSLAND
(To herself)

They do not need to be going

(MARTHA returns with fresh coffee for her FATHER)

MARTHA

Alfred is washing

MRS. HERSLAND
(To MR. HERSLAND)

He does not need to be going

MR. HERSLAND

Dont be a foolishness
He is going to the east
To help me in my business dealing

MRS. HERSLAND
(To herself)

David to eastern college
Alfred to help the father in his failing
But for him there is no helping
He will not succeed again
He is as he is, always and only beginning

MR. HERSLAND
(Having tasted new cup of coffee, mollified)
Never I take sugar in my coffee

DAVID
(To himself)

Two living and they wanted three
One now living
Only because two others
Had not been going on living
I did not, I did not know this thing

MR. HERSLAND
(To himself)

Martha staying

(Then, angrily to MARTHA*)*
Always holding my coat
Always sugar in my coffee

Mrs. Hersland
(To herself)

Little by little, I learned to know him
Little by little, I knew him in my feeling
Little by little
How far the nature in him would carry him

His way of loving
And loving coming out of him
His way of anger
And anger coming out of him
His way, his own way, of having fear in him

It is only repeating
Repeating in daily living

In the beginning of the ending of his middle living
His ways, all his ways
Come to be in him
Simple repeating

David

I am needing now to understand
Every minute in my living
What there is to me of meaning
In my having being
In my being one who needs it in me
To go on living

I am needing now to understand
What need there is to me for living

There were two before me
And I am living now
They needed three

MRS. HERSLAND

Alfred is not coming

DAVID

I will go for him
        (HE *leaves*)

MRS. HERSLAND
(To her HUSBAND*)*

The baby clothes
Are still in Alfreds closet
I will sort and wash them

MR. HERSLAND

Dont be a foolishness
They are not needed

MRS. HERSLAND

They are in the closet.

(MR. HERSLAND *sits again, at a distance from his*
WIFE. HE *studies her*)

MR. HERSLAND
(To himself)

She was a tender feeling
She was a gentle thing
In early living
She was a little like a flower inside me

She could a little affect me then
She could a little resist herself to me
And resisting, she was a little a joke to me

And then

MARTHA
*(Having finished with chores, stands at the table at a
distance from her FATHER, and addresses him)*

I do not know if it is ready yet for telling
One day I was alone
In a different part of town
Where I had gone to take a lesson in singing

And I saw a man hit a woman with an umbrella
And I was just then passing
And the woman had a red face
Partly in anger and partly in asking

And the man wanted the woman to know
That he wanted her to leave him alone
In a public street where people were passing

MARTHA

And then the moment happened in my living
It came to happen to me
That there was shock and a commotion in me
Strong
And the movement of the being in me
Was suddenly a little faster

And it came to be
Violent almost in me
When I saw this
A man hitting a woman on California Street
It made everything in me
Move together and faster
Than motion had ever been in me before

MR. HERSLAND

A little important for that
And then

MARTHA

He was beating the woman with an umbrella
And I had not any distinct feeling in me
About what I had been seeing
Not then and not now later
But it gave such motion to me
It gave direction to me

Mr. Hersland

A wife to me
Always outside of me
And not important

Martha
(Continues to her Father*)*
And I saw the man hitting the woman in the street
To rid himself of her and of her asking
And I saw this
And it was not a horror to me
I had no very certain feeling in me
It was confusion and excitement
It was nervousness in me

Mr. Hersland

A wife to me
A little important because of the children
She was full up with children for me
More and more resisting to me
More and more resisting for the children
And a little important
For that

And then

MR. HERSLAND

Then she was only the children
With no importance in her then for me
Only the children stronger and stronger
To do their own resisting

And then

MARTHA

I saw this
And it gave direction to me
And this man was for me
The ending of the living Ive been knowing

I would go to college
And now I am asking
I would go to college
I have this motion in me

And I will understand everything
And know the meaning of the living
And the feeling
The meaning and the living and the feeling
In men and women

I would go to college
And I would tell it then to my mother and my father
And I would ask them
And if they would make no objection
I would do this

MR. HERSLAND

And then

Then she was like eating and sleeping in me
Less and less a tender feeling
Less and less important to me
Less and less even a joke to me
Less and less part of the children to me
And more and more
Brushing her away from around me
Not in any way, in any way important

MARTHA

And it gave direction to me
I would tell this to my mother and my father
And I would ask them
If they are interested in this
In my doing this
In my going to college
In my having such a forward motion
I would ask them
If they are interested

(ALFRED *and* YOUNG DAVID *come in.* ALFRED *is in his
overcoat and hat, dressed stiffly, carrying a suitcase.*

Silence.

MARTHA *gives* DAVID *his suitcase and his hat, and
holds his overcoat for him)*

MR. HERSLAND
(Angrily)

Do not hold his coat
A daughter of mine
In my position

(Silence.

DAVID *takes his coat and puts it on himself.* BOTH
SONS *kiss their* MOTHER, DAVID *kisses his* FATHER.
ALFRED *stands at the door ready to leave)*

ALFRED
(To his FATHER*)*

Always to each one of us
Living together in the house with you
Always you were there
Outside of us to us
Part of the world to fear or fight
Always always for us

Sometimes you were pleasant for us
Sometimes playing
Angry, loving, using, mostly fighting
Always domineering and then dropping

Always we had it in us to be afraid of you
Always having such a fear in us of you
Never knowing it about you
How far the anger in you would drive you
And how far you lived your own life away from us

Then more and more we learned it of you
That mostly you were just filled up inside you
With angry feeling, impatient feeling, changing feeling
That you would not keep up anything against us
That soon you would be changing
Never carrying out against us
The last end of anger in you
And then there was not any more for us
Any single thing to fear from you

      (ALFRED *and* DAVID *leave.*

      MARTHA *snatches up her coat and runs out with them.*

      The THREE CHILDREN *arrive at center and far side of*
      stage from the house, ALL *facing different directions.*
      THEY *freeze)*

                MR. HERSLAND

Three
Three leaving
      *(*HE *gets up and paces. After a while,* HE *sits again)*

MRS. HERSLAND
(To herself)

Three leaving
When they were beginning
They were all my daily living
They were to me in me then
As they had been when I was bearing them
A part of me
As arms or heart were part of me
Then

I felt them
I took care of them
As I took care of my body
Out of which I had once made them
And so I always felt them
Then

Lost among them now
Frightened of them now
They are no longer of me now

GERTRUDE STEIN

Gentle scared little thing
Lost among them
The little important feeling dead in her

MRS. HERSLAND

Lost among them
They are not of me any more
Losing my body in losing them

GERTRUDE STEIN

A little one, a lost one
Lost to herself
They away from her inside her
A scared feeling in her

(*Lights down on* MR. *and* MRS. HERSLAND *and the house. The* THREE CHILDREN *are brilliantly illuminated in spotlights*)

Three leaving
Beginning middle living
Finding meaning
Finding living

END OF ACT TWO

Act Three

Act III

Scene 1

MARTHA, ALFRED *and* DAVID *are standing as* THEY
*were at the end of the previous act. The boxes are arranged in three separate structures, defining the three
areas used in the scene:* MARTHA's *western college,*
ALFRED's *house and* DAVID's *eastern college.*

MARTHA, ALFRED & DAVID
Little by little one is not so young
Still being young

GERTRUDE STEIN
Knowing a map
Then seeing the place
And knowing the actual roads are like the map
Astonishing and very gratifying

111

The same thing comes to those in living
Finding themselves beginning middle living
Looking like ones that once they knew in living

MARTHA, ALFRED & DAVID

Quickly one is not so young
Quite quickly one is not so young
And one is then still young

GERTRUDE STEIN

Astonishing and very gratifying
To some then even terrifying
And all kinds of feelings in between

Overwhelming then to know it
Really then inside them
That everything they once had seen
In older middle living
Is in them

MARTHA, ALFRED & DAVID

A little different and a little different
Seeing oneself a little and a little
Growing different

GERTRUDE STEIN

Three having in them
Beginning middle living

And like a map of anything
Find the changing in their being
Just like an exact description
Waiting

Martha, Alfred & David

A little different

> (Martha, Alfred *and* David *move toward their respective areas*)

Gertrude Stein

A history of three

Martha to western college
To study the rights and wrongs of women

Alfred to eastern living
To make his way

David to eastern college
To think and be

> (Martha, Alfred *and* David, *in their respective areas, sit as though writing letters.*
>
> Alfred *is with* Julia *and a little* Aunt, *who are being polite to one another.*

MARTHA *is with* PHILIP REDFERN, *who sits upright to
one side of her.*

DAVID *is alone)*

ALFRED

Liking it very much to be in pleasant living
And being a little in love
And that is almost still pleasant living
Even though the aunt with whom I am living
Is trying to be interfering
And is just a little breaking into for me
The pleasantness of pleasant living

MARTHA

Liking it very much to be in pleasant living
Sober earnest moral education
Completely democratic institution
Democracy the earnest aspiration
Of men and women, men and men, women and women
Comradeship among us all
Complete and genuine among us all
Liking it very much this pleasant living

ALFRED

Having some loving feeling in me
Some tender feeling in me
Playing music and having music in me

MARTHA

Men believing completely in the right
Of women to learning any occupation

ALFRED

Being a man now in my feeling
Remembering our pleasant family living
Not yet but soon aspiring will be
A very active thing in me

MARTHA

And also there is for us
Out of doors wandering
A kind of feeling
A kind of yearning
For beauty

ALFRED

Every one be good ones
Alfred Hersland

MARTHA

I have met Philip Redfern
Martha Hersland

He is a Virginian

DAVID

Eastern college too damn anxious to be safe
Why do they have to be so damned afraid
It aint so easy to hurt them as they think
Hitting them on the head wont kill them
Not if their heads are really hard

Afraid always afraid for their damn culture
Takes more than a man like me to kill it for them

GERTRUDE STEIN

Needing custom, passion, certainty of place
Wanting strong to be singular
In ways of living

Wanting and needing
Some such things

MARTHA & ALFRED

A pleasant thing to be in pleasant living

DAVID

Damn them
David Hersland

(Lights down on ALFRED *and* MARTHA*)*

Act III
Scene 2

GERTRUDE STEIN

Beginning
Only a little
From the outside
To realize him

(DAVID *gets up, puts on his cap and comes forward.*
PAULINE, *a young girl, joins him*)

Meets her, Pauline, me
The way it was with Leon sort of
Reading in back of trolley car
David in his tramping clothes and hat
Describe the one of Pablos

Look at each other
The way that big workman and I did

Pauline reading Frederick the Great
Regards him
He her
Stay on trolley into country
No remark all the way

He helps her off
They go walking

Three little boys leading
Bearing a bamboo with leaves on top
Sunshine, country life
Use Tarren country in the depths of sunshine

Regard each other all the way
Describe Leon's walk
Me
Describe us together

    (DAVID *and* PAULINE *abruptly change their action.*
    Lights change)

Midnight walks later
Lying out in the country
Et cetera

She and he both have their moments
But they know each other
And it is not worth while

She a bad one, make her so
He with a purpose

PAULINE
(Speaking throughout scene)
Now I have made you hate yourself again

DAVID
(Speaking throughout scene)
Dont you know you havent got any manners

PAULINE
I am awful sorry
But I have only been knowing you for three months
Just you wait a little
Then youll see em coming

DAVID
Then theyll come too much

GERTRUDE STEIN
Wanting to be feeling something
Wanting to be needing to be feeling something
And not clearly feeling that thing
Wanting to be almost a complete one in feeling that thing

PAULINE
No it isnt that

DAVID

Well then what is it
Why dont you say it
Why it isnt that

PAULINE

I dont know why I dont say it
I guess I just kind of dont want to

(*Light changes, and* DAVID *and* PAULINE *change their
action and place during:*)

GERTRUDE STEIN

Liking it very well all his living
To be finding every woman
Every kind of woman
A beautiful one in being loving

Wanting this thing all his living
Completely needing that every woman is a beautiful thing

DAVID

Damn fool, don't you know boys of that age are the most
dangerous a girl can fool with. Theyve got no sense of conse-
quences like there is in a man. And with a man, two men make
a woman safe, with boys the more, the more dangerous. They
got to show each other they aint afraid of anything. Didnt you
see that little one trying to touch your breasts. I cant see why
women have got to be such fools and not see things. Do you
suppose your being a lady would ever do you any good with
them. You women are certainly damn fools mostly.

GERTRUDE STEIN

She says go, go and I go
She says come, come and I come
She says come, come and I come
She says go, go and I go

Not really wanting
Really not wanting
Almost completely wanting
To be one needing to be going and coming
To be one needing to be coming and going

He was loving
He was one in a way
Doing submitting

>(*Lights have changed.*

>DAVID *and* PAULINE *have changed their action and their place*)

DAVID

You know I am working
I aint got time to loaf all day

No that dont satisfy you
Well probably youll like it better
If I just tell you I am bored to death
And so I am going

And that dont suit you either
All right make it the way you like it
It aint anything to me
But there is one thing theres no way of changing
Tomorrow morning I am going

GERTRUDE STEIN

Almost certain about this thing
About almost needing another one
Certainly often enough
Wanting to be completely needing another one

(Lights have changed.

DAVID *and* PAULINE *change their action)*

DAVID

I am a damn fool
I am a damn fool Pauline
There is no getting away from it
I am a damn fool

PAULINE

What do you want me to do

DAVID

Listen to me
I am a damn fool

GERTRUDE STEIN

Loving one then and in a way telling it to her
And in a way not really telling it to her

And certainly any one could know
That he and the one he was loving
Were ones who were not coming to be
Not she not he
Completely interested in that thing

And he was not then certain of this thing
And she was not then certain of this thing

(Lights have changed.

DAVID *and* PAULINE *have changed their action)*

DAVID

No not really ever in love with me
And not now ever in love with her

I got to the point and then retreated from it
And so now youre floating off with her

PAULINE

You dont want me to

DAVID

I dont want you to

PAULINE

But its only a moral thing for you
And you know it

DAVID

I supposed something like that was working in you

PAULINE

Let me know sometime what is happening to you

(SHE *leaves.*

DAVID *alone*)

GERTRUDE STEIN

He was almost always knowing this thing
That he was never completely needing one
Never completely needing any one

That he was one

ACT III
SCENE 3

Lights dim on DAVID, *come up brilliantly on* MARTHA *and* PHILIP REDFERN.

GERTRUDE STEIN

Meeting

PHILIP REDFERN

Mother was eager impetuous sensitive purposive

GERTRUDE STEIN

Running through the country

PHILIP REDFERN

Enthusiastic idealistic excitable vigorous

GERTRUDE STEIN

Plunging vigorously through the snow

125

PHILIP REDFERN

Determined rebellious poetic inspiring

GERTRUDE STEIN

Liking the cold air and the running
Filled with their health and youth and freedom

(THEY *come to rest*)

PHILIP REDFERN

She was my dear dear friend
   (HE *pauses, considers*)
Here it is new and strange and dangerous

MARTHA

Here it is simple and matter of course

PHILIP REDFERN

She had purpose and vigorous thinking
She taught me:
   (HE *cups his hands and shouts into the cold air*)
Be my champion
Philip, the champion of women
Sublime proof of the justice and poetry of living
The strength of the father
Soon in the son
To win liberty and hope for women

She fought him always without his knowing
But father was master in our house

GERTRUDE STEIN

The ardor of conceiving his being

The strength of the purpose
Of his dear dear friend inside him
Never touching his being

PHILIP REDFERN

You are a comrade and a woman
And here, it is the new world

MARTHA

Here it is simple and a matter of course

PHILIP REDFERN

I know it, I know it
It is the new world

The young man showed me yesterday
How it is here with men and women

But I do not understand
Was it right for him to do so yesterday
Throwing himself on the ground
And putting his head in your lap

It is strange

If it is right
I do not understand

Martha

I do not understand
What you do not understand

(Lights dim)

Gertrude Stein

Married

(Lights up. Philip faces Martha; She faces away from him)

Martha

I do not understand what has happened. Bruised and dazed, I am never certain whence comes the blow, how it is dealt, or why.

Gertrude Stein

I am copying now an old piece of writing

Philip Redfern

She is all that she had promised. She is strenuous and pure, but without grace and harsh. Our natures are separated by great gulfs.

Gertrude Stein

Copying an old piece of writing
Where I am using words that one time had real meaning

PHILIP REDFERN

She must suffer but what can I do. She is an inferior who
cannot learn the rules of the game.

GERTRUDE STEIN

Ways of seeing
I had once been using

(MISS DOUNOR *enters.*)

PHILIP REDFERN
(Speaking conversationally and fairly rapidly)

When Philip Redfern met Miss Dounor, she greeted him with
awkward shyness. He looked with interest at this new present-
ment of gentleness and intelligence. In his twenty-ninth year,
his world was still without worth or meaning. He longed for a
more vital human life.

GERTRUDE STEIN

Ways of feeling, knowing, thinking
I was once believing

MISS DOUNOR

Miss Dounor too had her ideals. Her life had been arranged
to leave her untouched and unattached, but in her there had
always been a desire for sordid life and the common lot.

GERTRUDE STEIN

Having a little shame
That such a writing is so young

(PHILIP REDFERN *embraces* MISS DUONOR *and* THEY
recline)

PHILIP REDFERN

He was willing to endure all pain for the ideal that filled him
with such deep unrest. In her he had found so fine a spirit that
no severity of suffering could deter him, knowing she too would
willingly pay high for the fresh vision that he brought her.

GERTRUDE STEIN

Always I must lose words I have once been using
Always I must lose words
But always in my living
I do not like throwing anything away

(PHILIP REDFERN *and* MISS DOUNOR *rise and leave*)

MARTHA

Martha could not escape the knowledge that something stronger
than community of intellectual interest bound her husband and
Miss Dounor together. She knew she was powerless to change
him. She could merely try to get evidence to condemn him.
She dreaded to obtain it. If she had it, she must act on it. He is
dishonorable, she said to herself, but found no comfort in this
thought.

(PHILIP REDFERN *returns*)

PHILIP REDFERN
It was the end of May, and one late afternoon Redfern came into the house and passed into his own study.

MARTHA
Martha sat in her room. Sadness had become stronger in her than desire.

PHILIP REDFERN
(Performing action indicated)
Redfern remained in his study a short while and then was called away.

(PHILIP REDFERN leaves)

MARTHA
(Performing action indicated)
As soon as he was out of sight, Martha rose and went into his room. She walked up to his desk. She opened his portfolio, and saw a letter in his writing. So eager was she to read it, she scarcely hesitated. She read it to the end. She had her evidence.

(PHILIP REDFERN returns. HE sees MARTHA with the letter in her hand. SHE sees him. Confusion. Freeze)

GERTRUDE STEIN
Writing books is like washing hair
You got to soap it a lot of times
Before you start to rinse it

(Blackout)

ACT III
SCENE 4

GERTRUDE STEIN

I am beginning now to go on
With my history of Julia Dehning and of Alfred Hersland
And their marrying

I am remembering everything I have been telling
I am always loving repeating
I am realizing kinds in men and women
I am realizing Alfred Hersland and Julia Dehning

I begin again
With what I know of being
And always now I will be using words
Having in me very real meaning

*(Lights have come up full on two areas: the Dehning
household, with* ALFRED HERSLAND *and the* DEHN-
INGS *assembled there, and in another place on* JULIA
*sitting at a dressing table. Her wedding gown and its
veil are on a clothes dummy.* SHE *is in her chemise,
very much be-ribboned and be-laced)*

THE DEHNINGS

Very pleasantly
Quite entirely decently
Not very aggressively
Pretty freely
Quite contentedly
Fairly advancedly
Thoroughly generously
Quite gaily
Pretty entirely cheerfully
Dehning family living

ALFRED HERSLAND

Knowing some
And being happy enough in living
And enjoying doing things
And coming to many with pleasant feeling

And every one a little curious
And touching and admiring this one
And always seeing this one as a tall one

GERTRUDE STEIN
The very pleasant feeling in Alfred Hersland

ALFRED HERSLAND & JULIA DEHNING
I am beginning now perhaps to be succeeding

(Lights dim slightly on the DEHNINGS, *come up full
on* JULIA*)*

JULIA DEHNING
I am learning how to show myself
Here and now
In careful dressing
As what I am and what I am wanting
As the final person I want to be
The person I finally am

I will learn to build it up in little pieces
Cutting and fitting and fitting and cutting and painting
And showing in careful dressing again and again
The final perfect person
The person I finally am

JULIA DEHNING & ALFRED HERSLAND
I am beginning now perhaps to be succeeding

(Lights dim on JULIA, *come up on* DEHNINGS*)*

ALFRED HERSLAND
(*Studying* MR. DEHNING)

Certainly he will be listening
He is needing more and more to be important
By being always ready to be listening

MR. DEHNING
(*Studying* ALFRED HERSLAND)

Certainly I will not be really listening
Certainly I will be listening
He is now in Dehning family living

A little uneven in him Alfred Hersland
Very full up inside him
But a little it is not the same all through him

ALFRED HERSLAND & JULIA DEHNING

Coming a little more to be succeeding

JULIA DEHNING

And when I see it clearly
The person I finally am
I will show in all my dressing
A little less than what I am
Less than the final perfect person
So as not to show to every one
As the person I finally am
A very strange or a queer one

Yes I will carefully show much less
In careful daily dressing
Than the final perfect person

                Julia Dehning & Alfred Hersland
Coming a little more to be succeeding

                        Alfred Hersland
Telling and repeating
Telling what I am needing

                            Mr. Dehning
Stammering
Telling it quite quickly
Not telling it
Seeming to be one not telling it
A little more a little less convincing
Not ever to completeness of convincing

                        Alfred Hersland
He is needing to be listening
To my telling and repeating

                Alfred Hersland & Julia Dehning
Soon it will begin to be convincing

                            Julia Dehning
Soon I will invent myself in dressing
And then create myself in daily living

By furnishing
By dressmaking
By decorating
By cleaning myself
By resting and reading
By being a good one
By learning everything

Not to be conspicuous in living
Only to be intelligent and elegant
I am learning I am feeling I am learning
How to be a finished thing

Little by little working
From something I am knowing
To little by little
Knowing something new

And finally knowing that thing
Finally coming to be
A finished thing
Finally finally sticking there
Sticking finished in that thing

(SHE *is dressed: gown, veil, gloves, flowers all in place.*
SHE *triumphs in the mirror)*

JULIA DEHNING & ALFRED HERSLAND
Coming to be completely now succeeding

MR. DEHNING

Soon yes I will be doing what he is needing
To be succeeding honestly in living
Sooner than he is ever really convincing

(ALFRED HERSLAND and JULIA DEHNING come forward and stand together as lights dim on both areas)

JULIA DEHNING & ALFRED HERSLAND

Coming to be completely now succeeding

(As light fades on them)

GERTRUDE STEIN

And Alfred Hersland in him not believing
Not very much hardly at all believing
He will ever come to finally succeeding
When finally he is a finished thing

ACT III
SCENE 5

Lights up on MR. AND MRS. DEHNING *in their house. In another place, lights up on* ALFRED *and* JULIA HERSLAND *in their house.*

MR. DEHNING

I am not going into any house
Where Alfred Hersland is living
I am not, I am never

Certain now and sure

ALFRED HERSLAND
(Shouting)

Damn your people

141

JULIA HERSLAND
(Furious)
No honest human being can believe
That any one like you is living
That any man that is a man
Loves anything but honest living

ALFRED HERSLAND
Not any one, not any one believes
I am not honest except your father damn him
(Pounding on the table)
Damn him damn you damn all of you

JULIA HERSLAND
(Shouting too)
Dont pound

ALFRED HERSLAND
I pounded and I meant to pound it in

MR. DEHNING
I am not going into any house
Where Alfred Hersland is living
You, you are going
You are seeing Julia
Well and good

But I am not, I am never

I am certain now and sure

JULIA HERSLAND

For me to think it in myself as real
That any one belonging to my kind
Could lie or cheat
Could do a crooked thing

The thing you did
It could never
Every man I could belong to ever
Was good and straight
They had this simply so
In a good sane simple world

ALFRED HERSLAND

Damn your father damn you

JULIA HERSLAND
(Shouting louder)

Dont pound

MR. DEHNING

Never will I talk about this thing
Not to you not to George not to Julia
But I am certain and convinced
He is not honest
Ever

I will not speak to him
I will not see him

Never

(Blackout)

ACT III
SCENE 6

GERTRUDE STEIN

A little in pieces
Almost
Not entirely
Almost whole ones to my feeling
Alfred Hersland Julia Hersland
Knowing loving

(Lights up on JULIA *and* ALFRED HERSLAND *in their house, not facing each other)*

ALFRED HERSLAND

Harsh and crude and eager in her fighting

Not not really
No not really ever a harsh one
Sometimes a sort of sweetness in her fighting

145

JULIA HERSLAND

The fear he has in him in loving
Afraid that I will not attack enough to win him
If he is too successful in resisting

ALFRED HERSLAND

She does not fight for winning or for losing
But only to be fighting and attacking
Always giving herself the right
To be harsh or crude or eager
However she wants to do it in her fighting

JULIA HERSLAND

Uneasy and afraid
Of using the resisting in him
Always afraid

Slowly coming to understand

ALFRED HERSLAND

Stupid and crude
She has not any sense for living
Stupid and crude

Slowly coming to understand

ALFRED & JULIA HERSLAND

Coming to be needing
To have each other
Coming to be needing

(Lights change, and ALFRED *and* JULIA *change their action and place, during:)*

GERTRUDE STEIN

I am loving
I am loving every kind of loving
I am loving just now very much all loving

ALFRED & JULIA HERSLAND

Coming to be needing
To have each other
For loving and for living

GERTRUDE STEIN

I am feeling now with lightness and delight
With conviction, acquiescing, curious feeling
All the ways there are of having loving

I am telling now with lightness and delight
A kind of loving

(Lights up full, and ALFRED *and* JULIA *begin their new action)*

JULIA HERSLAND

A quivering
Completely loving
Completely quivering
All loving and certain of being really loving

ALFRED HERSLAND

How much how little I am loving
I am never knowing
It is wonderful
To see someone completely certain
Of having completely quivering loving

JULIA HERSLAND

Quivering into loving
Quicker than chain-lightning
Attacking trembling

ALFRED HERSLAND

Resisting simple

JULIA HERSLAND

Attacking quivering

ALFRED HERSLAND

Resisting vacant

JULIA HERSLAND

Attacking rushing

ALFRED HERSLAND

Resisting stubborn

JULIA HERSLAND

Attacking piercing

Alfred Hersland

Resisting yielding

Julia Hersland

Attacking mystic

Alfred Hersland

Resisting solemn

Julia Hersland

Attacking planned

Alfred Hersland

Resisting fearful

Julia Hersland

Attacking troubled

Alfred Hersland

Resisting timid

Julia Hersland

Attacking stupid

Alfred Hersland

Resisting embracing

Muddy
Engulfing
A deep sinking and emerging
A slow entering and a slow emerging
Nervous when the slowness goes too fast

> *(Lights change, and* Alfred *and* Julia *change their action and their place during:)*

GERTRUDE STEIN

Liking loving
Liking all the ways one can have of loving
Slowly this has come to be in me
That any way of being a loving one
Is interesting and not unpleasant to me
I like now every way there is of having loving

(Lights up full. ALFRED *and* JULIA *begin their new
action)*

ALFRED HERSLAND

A thing

JULIA HERSLAND

I and a thing

ALFRED HERSLAND

The dirt of things
A slow sure feeling
That things are made of earth
Slow feeling
The dirt of things

JULIA HERSLAND

I in relation to a thing
The smell the beauty the use of things
Everything relating things to things

ALFRED HERSLAND & GERTRUDE STEIN

Things existing
Really ordinarily existing
In any field
In any road
In any place
In any garden
Like any dirt
Things have existing being

JULIA HERSLAND

I feel I see I need I use
All things in all relations
Feeling things in their relation
With the poignance of sensation

ALFRED & JULIA HERSLAND

Certainly coming to be needing
To have each other
Certainly for living

(Lights change, and ALFRED *and* JULIA *change their action and their place during:)*

GERTRUDE STEIN

Almost entirely
Not completely
Whole ones to my feeling
Almost entirely knowing
Alfred Hersland and Julia Hersland in married loving

(Lights up full. ALFRED *and* JULIA *begin their new
action)*

ALFRED HERSLAND

Sometimes I am wondering

How can they be so certain
They are really loving
How can they be so certain

It is wonderful
That such a one can have completely
Energy and certainty in loving
That such a one can have
Poignant loving feeling

I am wondering
And then I am adoring
One really having poignant loving feeling

How can I be certain
That the feeling in me is completely loving feeling
Really I am not certain
That I believe in loving
That I believe in honest living
That I believe that any one is a good one

How is one then certain

How does one know in living
Goodness, honest feeling, honest thinking
I know it is going on in me
I know it is going on in them
But I am not believing

And how then is one certain
That goodness, loving, honest feeling
Is in them
And how is one not certain

And what is then the satisfaction
Of having been, of being, of going on
When one is not then certain
That loving, goodness, honest feeling
Is in them
And one is not then certain

It is to some a difficult thing
To be certain
That they have loving, goodness, honest living
That they have thinking
That they have feeling
Really going on in them

JULIA HERSLAND

Having honesty in living
Having Dehning family living

And stamping that thing
Stamping that thing very certainly

Always I am a hopeful one
Always I am learning everything

And yet not really hearing feeling seeing
Anything any way ever changing
The attacking I have all my living in me

ALFRED & JULIA HERSLAND

Always coming to be needing
Coming to be succeeding
In not succeeding

(Lights begin to dim slowly on ALFRED *and* JULIA*)*

GERTRUDE STEIN

Married living going on
Partly failing
Partly succeeding

And I am not now finding it to me
At all an interesting thing
Telling any more about the being
In the loving and the married living
Of Julia Hersland and of Alfred Hersland

Leave them

(Lights fade on ALFRED *and* JULIA HERSLAND*)*

I am going on describing
Old and disillusioned ones
I am realising old ones
One and then another one
I am going on describing
Old men, old women in their dying

(Lights have come up on MRS. HERSLAND *and* MRS. DEHNING, *in their houses, both women ailing.* MR. HERSLAND *sits, not facing his wife, then goes out.* MR. DEHNING *sits, not facing his wife)*

MRS. HERSLAND

Old ones
Old and sick ones
Body living

MRS. DEHNING

Having to look at
Having to care for
Each for the others
Old ones troubles

MRS. HERSLAND

Old man old woman coming to have in us
Old body wearing

MRS. DEHNING

Making each other do what we want each other to do
What is right for each
What is good for the other
Teaching the other a good right way
Not to be dying

MRS. HERSLAND

And always having to see
Each one and the other
The always shrinking away
The small one left for dying

MRS. DEHNING

Coming too much to stay inside me
To want more living

Mrs. Hersland

Afraid
Failing living
Dying

(Lights down on Hersland *house)*

Mrs. Dehning

Not a very long living in me
A long living
Most that I remember of it
Married living

Nice and good and pleasant and successful
Married living

Careful generous kindly man
Good husband to his wife
Good enough father to his children
And always could be made by me
To do what I would have him

It would have been better
That he had been the first to be the dead one
Not any man
Not this man I have known all my living
Can not be managed to be married by a woman

And then there will be trouble for the children
It would have been better
If he had been the first

Devoted man
A good one
But he will be needing a woman to fill him

The children will not want, for their sake
That he should marry some one
He should have been the first to be the dead one

MR. DEHNING
A longer living in me, well, yes, well
She will be the first to be the dead one

A woman by me, after, one to fill me
Some woman, any woman, will be by me
Old men try to keep warm

(Lights dim)

ACT III
SCENE 7

Lights come up on the HERSLAND *house.* MARTHA *and* MR. HERSLAND *are in mourning clothing.* MR. HERSLAND'S *black silk hat is on the table.* MARTHA *is preparing food.*

MR. HERSLAND

Is David coming
Is he Alfred coming

MARTHA

They are coming

MR. HERSLAND

When

(No answer from MARTHA*)*

159

She died away
But mostly they forgot about her
    (HE *gets up and paces*)
Are we ready for leaving

MARTHA

Yes

MR. HERSLAND

When

MARTHA

After the burying

MR. HERSLAND

When will they be here
    (HE *paces, then walks out of the room*)

MARTHA

Busy with beginning

Always to commence a new beginning
To be big again inside him

Always to the ending
Busy with beginning

Being with him
Always afraid
Caring for him
Always afraid
Till the last ending
Always afraid

Always the sugar in the coffee
Always holding the coat
Always not remembering
Always afraid

Every minute of my living is the same whole one
When I am older
When I am shrunken
And doing fighting still
When he is ended
And I begin again
And then begin again
Now and then and always
Fighting for the cause of women
A little crazy and a little crazier
As they are saying
As they will be saying

Always in beginning
Always in ending
Doing fighting

I am knowing
I will be knowing
It is the same
Every minute of my living
Is the same whole one

(MR. HERSLAND *returns*)

MR. HERSLAND

Are they here
Are we ready

MARTHA

They will be here

MR. HERSLAND

When

(Lights dim)

ACT III
SCENE 8

GERTRUDE STEIN

And leave them

When the world is so existing to my feeling
That all repeating is in pieces
That only a piece and pieces are repeating
That every one I am remembering
Is to me a piece of being
There is not any satisfaction in my feeling
Of having completion, of having anything a whole one
There is not any use
Not any use at all then to my being
Of going on existing
So that everything can keep on with repeating
Only a piece and pieces of its being
Not any use at all then to me

In going on existing
And this is now the real state of my feeling

Knowing each one as a whole one
Each one as of a kind of all the kinds
Of all the men and women ever living
Is in my feeling an important thing
Always an important thing to me
Every one himself inside him
Every one a kind of men and women
I am important in this thing

And so I am going on and going on describing
One and then another one
And connections then between them
And I am hurrying
And I am crowding
And then I am not certain
And then I am wondering
Is it perhaps not really, not completely
Perhaps it is not completely an important thing
Perhaps not anything is inspiriting in living
Not anything inspiriting to be a live one

Always dead is dead
Dead is dead and to be certain
That such a thing, that dead is dead
Is existing
The knowing dead is dead
The certain knowing that a dead one is a dead one

Always there has been in me
The being very much afraid
Always it is to me a sombre thing
The certain knowing that a dead one is a dead one
Always to me a sombre thing in living

I am going on
Going on and ending
Telling my understanding of this one
Of this lonely sad one
And so ending

And I am saddened with this thing
Sad and disillusioned with this thing
That not any one really knows
No others really know
What I have known and know
In living

Knowing disillusionment in living
Completely realizing that no one can believe
Not any one can believe as I do
About anything

Many many have in them
The disillusion of this thing
And so they say
They will write for themselves and strangers

I go on now to this ending
I will be ending
    (DAVID *becomes visible on an empty stage*)
Telling of this one
And doing something new
Doing this new thing

I will tell the life inside him
Only the life inside him
Nothing more of the outside
Only the living the being the knowing
As I know it
Deep inside him

    (DAVID *remains brilliantly spotlighted throughout the
    scene. The rest of the stage, even when lighted, is dim*)

DAVID
    (*A very young child recalling an even younger time*)
Living then
A little one
Gentle enough and active enough and happy enough
And earnest enough and quick enough and eager enough

GERTRUDE STEIN
Beginning living
And then going on being living
A little bigger one
And then a little a bigger one

DAVID

And careful enough and weak enough and doing enough
To be one being a little one being then living

GERTRUDE STEIN

Beginning being living
David Hersland
And coming to be a dead one
At the ending of beginning middle living

DAVID

Beginning living
And very well taken care of then
A very natural thing beginning living

GERTRUDE STEIN

Beginning living
David Hersland coming to be a dead one
A history of the dying he was doing
The dying he did when he was living
The dying he was doing in being in living

David Hersland
A history of living being dying

DAVID

Beginning living
A very little one

(MARTHA *and* ALFRED *as children, and the children
who played with* ALFRED—*Act II, Scene 1—are with*
DAVID, *and are playing*)

GERTRUDE STEIN
A little remembering a little a bigger one

DAVID
(Remaining apart from the playing CHILDREN)
Remembering and not completely interested
Remembering from then
Not at all minding remembering

GERTRUDE STEIN
Pretty nearly liking some things then
Playing some, being a younger one
Pretty nearly entirely liking it

DAVID
(Playing the CHILDREN'S *game, but still apart from
them*)
Playing some and jumping
Doing jumping
And jumping well enough
And jumping then
And doing it so wonderfully
And I am jumping
And not any one is jumping
A longer distance than I am jumping

And landing somewhere
And not important to be knowing
Where I am going to be landing
In beginning jumping
And very satisfying to be jumping
And jumping and not caring where one lands

GERTRUDE STEIN

Jumping from a place and landing

(*The chorus of* CHILDREN *disappear.* MARTHA *and*
ALFRED *play apart,* DAVID *lies down and occupies
himself*)

DAVID

Being a young one smelling
Certainly doing smelling
And smelling oneself when smelling something
Some are interested in smelling and then completely remem-
bering

I am not really interested in remembering from smelling

GERTRUDE STEIN

Being a young one and dreaming

(MARTHA, ALFRED *and* DAVID *again lying in the
orchard of their house, as* THEY *did in Act I, Scene 4)*

DAVID

Being a young one
And being one dreaming not of anything
And liking being dreaming
Sometimes dreaming about something
And sometimes dreaming not of anything
Liking being a young one being living
Certainly sometimes, almost always, liking

GERTRUDE STEIN

Liking being one going on being living
And living till the ending of beginning middle living
Knowing everyone will sometime be a dead one
In a way not at all completely knowing
In a way turning then away
From knowing dying

(DAVID *is once again apart from* MARTHA *and* AL-FRED)

DAVID

Dying
Not very exciting
A little terrifying
Quite interesting
Not happening, certainly not happening

GERTRUDE STEIN

David Hersland then
Not wanting not needing knowing dying

DAVID
(Determinedly pushing aside the idea of death)
Or needing to be completely forgotten
Or making it that one is wanting to be certain
That being a dead one is not happening
Or one is finding interesting
Or one is then a good deal forgetting

GERTRUDE STEIN
David Hersland then
Not wanting knowing dead is dead
Not wanting knowing then

DAVID
(Passionate, defiant hosannah)
It can be known, this thing
It can be known in a way every day
That one is being living
It can be known every day

It can be known all day
It can be known all of living every day

All of living I am knowing
In a way all of living
I know it every day
All of living every day I know I am being living
I know in a way
I am being living every day

It can be known
All of being living

GERTRUDE STEIN

A description of one living
Of his being, of his talking, of his listening
Of his eating, of his dying
Of his going on being living
Very much a history of one

> (MARTHA, ALFRED *and* DAVID *have gone into their*
> *house.* THEY *gather, with* MR. *and* MRS. HERSLAND,
> *as in Act I, Scene 5.* ALFRED *and* MR. HERSLAND *are*
> *in the same positions as when* THEY *were shouting and*
> *pounding on the table.* DAVID *is apart from the* FAM-
> ILY *group)*

DAVID

Angry feeling again and again in family living
And sometimes one in family living
Needing angry feeling to be existing
Or not wanting angry feeling ever existing
Completely not wanting angry feeling
And sometimes having angry feeling
About angry feeling being existing

One, in one to one, has not in any way
Power of doing anything
When that one is an angry one
Is not convincing, is not injuring
In one to one
Filled up with furious angry feeling
Not convincing, not injuring, not pleasing
That one with angry furious feeling

    (DAVID *runs out of the house, paces center stage.*
    Lights fade on house)

Angry feeling and then not feeling anything
And then a troubled one

And then troubled with this thing
With being a troubled one
And then not always certain
About anything about this thing
About being a troubled one
And wondering then about any one
Being a troubled one
And then quite clearly deciding about oneself
About oneself in being a troubled one

(Lights again come up on the house. The HERSLANDS *are gathered as in Act I, Scene 7:* MRS. HERSLAND *propped on the sofa with pillows, ailing;* MR. HERS- LAND, *at a distance from her, watching her;* MARTHA *trying to address her father;* ALFRED *at the door, ready to leave.* DAVID *remains center stage, apart from them)*

GERTRUDE STEIN

Until learning
And knowing then that two
Had not been going on living

DAVID
(Tormented outcry)

I do ask some
I do ask some
I would ask everyone
I do ask some if they would like it
If they would very much dislike it
If they would make a joke of it
If they would make a tragic thing of it
I do ask some
If they have any feeling about any
About some such thing
   (Squatting, hunched, clutching his arms in self-embrace, morbidly pleased)

And soon liking thinking about feeling
Certainly liking thinking about feeling
About some such thing
  (With bitter determination)
And needing to be certain
Every minute in my being
Needing being living

Wanting to be living
Needing to be living
To myself inside me
  (The pain of his uncertainty gradually becoming over-
  whelming)
Needing knowing living in myself inside me
Needing to be certain I was one being living
To myself inside me
And needing
Wanting
Needing
To have some
To have others
To be certain of this thing
To be certain I am one being living
To have some to have others to be certain I am living
To myself inside me

Needing to have others to be certain I am living
In myself
Inside me

GERTRUDE STEIN
Of his coming to be thinking
Of his coming to be a dead one

His coming to be thinking
Again and again and very often
Of coming to be a dead one

(DAVID *is sitting on the ground, as though writing*)

GERTRUDE STEIN & DAVID
Writing down then every day
The being of a troubled one
A troubled and a sad one

(A *long pause, during which* MARTHA *and* ALFRED
leave the house, and stand as THEY *did at the end of
Act II, each facing in a different direction*)

And liking certainly liking
Liking thinking about feeling
About some such thing

GERTRUDE STEIN
(As DAVID *is writing)*

Very many being living
Are often saying thank you to some one
Very many not saying thank you to any one

David Hersland not saying thank you to any one
David Hersland not saying thank you to any one

*(*DAVID *gets up, and takes his position as at the end of Act II, facing in a different direction from* MARTHA *and* ALFRED*)*

GERTRUDE STEIN & DAVID

David Hersland knowing one is not so young
Still being young

(Dim pools of light appear all over the stage. MARTHA *and* ALFRED *leave.* PAULINE *and* OTHER YOUNG PEOPLE *appear and move in and out of the pools of light.* DAVID *watches them but does not join them)*

DAVID

Sometimes with one
Sometimes with six
Sometimes with more than six
Sometimes with two
Sometimes with three

Going on being living
Where certainly very many come together
And being one with them
In a way not one with them

(The YOUNG PEOPLE *stop their movement, are in
groups of twos and threes, sit, stand, talk*)

And wanting to be living then
Completely understanding something then
Completely clearly thinking then
And needing to be thinking everything
To a completed thing

(DAVID *has moved into the midst of the* YOUNG PEO-
PLE, *and* SOME *are attending to him, as though* HE *is
explaining something to them*)

And coming to be making thinking
A pretty a transparent thing
A thing so clear it does not have
Beginning then or middle then or ending
And so a little a confusing thing
Confused and not completely clear a thing

(*Lights begin to fade on the* GROUPS OF YOUNG PEO-
PLE, *as a spotlight gradually illuminates* PAULINE.
Little by little, the YOUNG PEOPLE *listening to* DAVID
turn away)

And certainly then needing to be feeling
That any woman living is in some way
A really beautiful a sparkling thing

GERTRUDE STEIN

Thinking, talking, listening
Wanting to be needing

DAVID

Knowing some
And in a way one with them
In many ways not one with them

Not completely interesting to them
In being one wanting to be loving
A sparkling and completely beautiful one

(The stage is now dark, with PAULINE *and* DAVID *in spotlights.* THEY *are distant from one another, and* THEY *do not move.*

DAVID *undergoes the sequence of his feelings during the course of his affair with* PAULINE, *beginning with the anticipation of the Shulamite and ending as* DAVID *alone)*

Some one coming to be loving
And certainly now listening
And certainly I am knowing
Knowing this one listening
Being certain in a way
Of this one coming to be loving
And certainly almost doing
Almost completely doing loving
And certainly this one loving
Will be completely listening

And in a way, certainly
In not doing completely listening
In not completely loving
In not completely listening to one
To all of one
In a way not really loving
Not really listening

> *(The dim pools of light appear again. The* Young
> People *walk in criss-cross patterns, and David, in the
> midst of them, is momentarily lost among them. The*
> Young People *gradually disappear.* David, *alone, is
> sitting at a small table center stage)*

Gertrude Stein

Quietly enough living then
Teaching some then
Very nearly completely teaching some
Quietly enough being one being living

Being
Being remembered and forgotten
Going on being living
Going on dying
Coming to be a dead one
Quietly enough
A description of that thing

David

Quite quiet one, quite gentle one
Quite quiet one needing to be making something
Needing to be writing, needing to be doing something
To be a thing leading to another thing
Which would then be a thing failing
Failing to be a complete thing, a whole thing
And then not needing being anything
Not having been a beautiful thing
        (He *gets up and paces about*)
Quite quiet one, quite gentle one
Always wanting to be certain
That this one, that some one, that almost any one
Is one who is really existing

Myself to myself inside me, one
Is certainly not existing
And certainly one is wondering
And certainly then not wondering

Completely thinking
Completely knowing about thinking
Thinking about thinking

Not completely interested
Not completely understanding
Not completely needing going on existing
      (DAVID *is again sitting at the table, leaning forward,*
      hands clasped)

                    GERTRUDE STEIN
Thinking, feeling
Something in him feeling being
Completely different from any other one
Feeling being such a one

One deciding
Deciding dying

      (DAVID *has propped his head back, slumps and sits*
      limply)

                    DAVID
Not needing being one being certainly
Needing another one

Not needing to be one remembering
That any one can come to be a dead one

Not completely needing being living

Not really interested in being one
Not any longer living

Deciding not
   (HE *is silent.* HE *remains limp. Dead*)

      GERTRUDE STEIN
Not beginning again in being living
Not being one being living
At the ending of beginning middle living

Dead

He had come to be a dead one
At the ending of beginning middle living

Dead

He had come to be a dead one
He came then to be a dead one
He had come
He had come
To be a dead one

   (SOME *who knew* DAVID *appear, move slowly about in
pools of light, move in and out*)

Not completely needing
Needing being a dead one
Not one needing
Not any one had been needing
Had been at all needing
Had been wanting to be needing
Really at all needing
Not any one had been wanting to be needing
That he had come to be a dead one
He had not needed
It was not
It was not
A needed thing

He had come to be a dead one

THOSE WHO KNEW OF DAVID

Some remembering this thing
That he had come to be a dead one
Some indignant about this thing
That he had come to be a dead one
Some regretting this thing
That he had come to be a dead one
Some vague about this thing
That he had come to be a dead one
Some not remembering this thing
That he had come to be a dead one
Some certain he was dead
That he had come to be a dead one

Some interested in that thing
That he had come to be a dead one
Some wondering about this thing
That he had come to be a dead one
Some not knowing this thing
That he had come to be a dead one
Some feeling it a strange thing
That he had come to be a dead one
Some certain he was dead
That he had come to be a dead one
Some certain it was an important thing
That he had come to be a dead one
Some not certain it was an important thing
That he was then not being a living one
That he had come to be a dead one

Gertrude Stein

Any one could be not very constantly remembering
His being a dead one
His having been a living one

Those Who Knew of David

Any one could remember this thing
His having been a dead one
His having been a living one

> (David, *dead, is sometimes visible, sometimes con-cealed, among those who are moving slowly about. Lights dim.* Gertrude Stein *is alone.*)

GERTRUDE STEIN

Living, dying, being and existing
Always and always
The hymn of repetition

Living dying being and existing
Every one who ever was or is or will be living
Has been knowing and remembering
Is knowing and remembering
Will know and will remember
Some such thing

Living dying being and existing
I believe in things as earth
I believe in all repeating
I believe in things existing
As Cezanne as Caliban believed in them

Always and always
This is my way
Always and always
This will be my way
Always and always
I feel it and I write it

Living dying being and existing
Always and always
The hymn of repetition

END